Leland G Olson was a farm kid, not poor, but he learned about scratching with the chickens. This book had a lengthy gestation process, forming in his mind for decades while he lived through almost every aspect involved with a severe spinal cord injury. He credits his survival to a loving creator and strength received from the memories of those who prepared the way for him. Their spirits spoke to him and encouraged him to press onward.

To my loving family, who still do not believe I can write.

Leland G Olson

PLIGHTS AND PERILS OF PERSEVERING PIONEERS

AUSTIN MACAULEY PUBLISHERS™

LONDON • CAMBRIDGE • NEW YORK • SHARJAH

Ordering Information:
Quantity sales: special discounts are available on quantity purchases by corporations, associations, and others. For details, contact the publisher at the address below.

Publisher's Cataloging-in-Publication data
Olson, Leland G
Plights and Perils of Persevering Pioneers

ISBN 9781645753940 (Paperback)
ISBN 9781645753957 (Hardback)
ISBN 9781645753964 (ePub e-book)

Library of Congress Control Number: 2020903266

www.austinmacauley.com/us

First Published (2020)
Austin Macauley Publishers LLC
40 Wall Street, 28th Floor
New York, NY 10005
USA

mail-usa@austinmacauley.com
+1 (646) 5125767

I would like to acknowledge Austin Macauley Publishers Ltd. They may let me dwell for a spell in the authors' community. I must acknowledge my family members who have gone on before me, leaving a legacy of faith, hope, and pride. Loving families are the glue that binds great nations together.

"What kind of people live around here?
The same kind you had where you came from."

– Unknown

Chapter 1
The Atlantic Crossing

There was an exodus of biblical proportion, as thousands of people left the Scandinavian countries in the 1870s. Brave, adventurous, and some hungry people wanted to go to that new land of milk and honey. The word from earlier travelers came back it created an urgency, a sense of haste to get to that land and stake claim to homestead, then improve land, that would become their own. A mass of humanity, tempered by a hard life, now seeking a better, new way to live. Louie and Anna Karlson left Norway in 1877. They traveled to Liverpool, England, then boarded a Cunard Line Steamship for the uncertain, thirteen-day trip to cross the wide Atlantic Ocean. They were fearless newlyweds, not yet owners of extensive personal property. Everything they owned was with them, being carried or packed in a steamer trunk. A strong, unshakable faith was carried on their happy faces, in their hearts and actions.

To them, it was a cheerful, romantic and uneventful crossing. In their minds, it was their personal honeymoon cruise, the tickets were $21.00 each. The big boat was a couple 100 miles (ca. 161 kilometers) off the Massachusetts coast when smooth sailing weather took a radical change.

The ship encountered a huge, powerful nor'easter. Large as it was, that ship bobbed around like a fishing cork, or a small skiff, on the churning water. Gigantic waves pounded it mercilessly as the waves resembled mountains. That worthy ship slowly labored up and over each mountain only to be quickly plunged down into the next valley, thrilling or possibly petrifying the wealthy passengers on the upper deck.

Poor immigrants traveling below deck received the full booming, crashing, and amplified sound of the ship being battered by each heavy wave. Below deck there was little ventilation, the air was hot and sticky, many unwashed bodies all added to the calamity that the storm now presented. People became seasick, the conversations revealed minds were filled with doubt about the decision to travel to that new, far-off land.

It was enough to scare the passengers into thoughts of death, maybe contemplating leaving that sinking ship as a heavenly body. Some with doubts about eternity, saw a fiery abyss, and not the boiler room. A few, just descending to the deep, dark depths of the ocean, while trapped in the bowels of the ship. To make shattered nerves worse, travel was near iceberg-hidden waters. There were times when other steamships could be viewed traveling in the opposite direction. A portion of that trip was made in fog, the eastbound lanes and the westbound lanes paralleled quite close in some waters, making it dangerous in the dense fog. The captain cheerfully announced one foggy morning not to worry, "that is what foghorns are for," as he made a proud, loud and long test blast on his prized musical instrument.

Anna was nearing the time to give birth and said to Louie, "Your father never did like me, you knew that?"

Louie replied, "No, I did not know that."

"Your father caught me out walking in the woods one day and he walked with me. He said in a tone of voice I've never heard him use, it was almost a hissing sound, 'Babies are supposed to take nine months, didn't you know that?' He could see I was pregnant, that outburst really surprised and shocked me. He asked me, 'Are you going to take our Louie and leave Norway, now that you have him?'

"Anna, please do not let that bother you, he will get over it in time."

"My father has very strict, old-fashioned ways. If your father had it to do over, he would never send you into Oslo by yourself again."

"That might be true, but what is done is history, and we will all make the most of it. The important thing is that I love you and my father will learn to love you."

This carnival-like roller-coaster cruise had started to make him a bit seasick. The air was hot and stifling for this fearless, strong, red-haired Viking *sailor*. It was making him think seriously about being sick and losing that meager breakfast of gruesome gruel. As the trip was nearing its end, Anna cried out, "Louie, go find Ingeborg Johansson. I think the baby is coming. She told me to come and get her when it was time, I'm sure the time has come." He searched and soon found Ingeborg and asked her to come quick as his wife was in labor. They were in a location that wasn't quite so crowded.

Ingeborg examined her, then replied, "Oh my, I think the baby is coming the wrong way."

She told Louie, "Quickly now, pick your wife up and turn her body over then hold her, I believe the baby will turn itself inside of her." Louie looked at her with a puzzled expression on his face but obeyed her stern command. He held his crying wife very tightly and slowly turned her over. It was only a short time but seemed like an eternity with Anna moaning and crying in his arms. Ingeborg shouted, "Praise the Lord! It worked. Your baby is coming into this world, the right way now." It was only a few moments before the crying of a new baby was heard. A cheer went out from the passengers in that part of the ship. A new Norwegian-American was born aboard ship that day, a baby boy was born, they named him Christian. He was a big, healthy baby.

Chapter 2
New York to Michigan

The Karlson family was slowly processed through immigration at Ellis Island in New York. It took hours. To conserve what little money they had in their small nest egg, they decided to leave for Michigan as soon as possible. There were several first and second cousins already working in the copper mines to help them get settled when they arrived. Most men had worked in the mines of Norway and had found similar safety standards. The tons of ore delivered per man was the bottom line for everybody in the world. Their ancestors in Norway were among the most primitive copper miners, using burning torches that consumed the oxygen they were breathing. New explosive materials were developed along with mining techniques which increased production dramatically. Safety standards were being placed on the back burner in many instances, once a miner always a miner, danger or not. Most of the miners in Norway had fathers who were farmers. They grew up loving the life on the farm and had dreams of owning their own farm sooner or later. It created a great incentive to work hard in the mines to save money. The goal was to continue going west where they could homestead land and improve it until it became their own. With dreams like that, a strong growing nation grew and prospered on the backs of energetic God-fearing people.

Many of the immigrants from Europe worked in the copper mines of Michigan before they migrated along the edge of Lake Superior to Minnesota, as iron mines were flourishing there. Iron ore was being shipped from Duluth through Lake Superior, then to all parts of the world. It was open-pit mining, much different working conditions than the underground copper mines. Many people stayed in Northern Minnesota and farmed land. They milked a few cows, raised a few hogs, grew corn, wheat, and oats, raised sugar beets and rutabagas, which the cattle ate with gusto in the cold winters of the North. The Finns had a recipe for rutabaga pudding, some might turn up their noses, but it was a very tasty dish. The lakes had huge lake trout. Minnesota became known as the land of 10,000 lakes for a good reason; there was a lake every few miles all the way across. The densely forested land had wolves, deer, and moose. Trapping furs was a prosperous living for those who didn't want to work in the mining business.

Louie, Anna and Chris, started out by train a few days after arriving in New York, they traveled by train to the Upper Peninsula of Michigan. Louie immediately went to work in a copper mine, being a seasoned miner in Norway. He considered the pay more than adequate, but Anna felt the work was far too dangerous for any amount of wage. She kept telling him, "Let's go to Dakota Territory as so many others have done before us and start farming." She said, "I fear you will be killed beneath that foggy, cold lake if the mine should collapse. I lay awake at night thinking about you being trapped under the icy water. Our baby, Chris, is healthy and growing fast. I think it would be a good place for him to grow up on a farm, with brothers and sisters."

"Okay, Anna, I will work here for another six months. We will save every penny of our money, then move to Dakota Territory early in the spring. You do realize, we will not have anything to start with, no home, nothing. Just as others did, we must homestead some land, then start making improvements on it. The first thing will be to dig a hole into the side of a hill like a badger or a fox, or build a sod house to live in. After a year or two, when we have some money from crops, then we will build a wood frame house or even a stone house."

"Louie, you don't paint a very bright picture. I see nothing good for us to look at, you would never be an artist."

"Ah, my wife of little faith makes jokes too! Anna, you must admit that our lives together are brightly colored with hope and most of all love.

"Anna, the reason I want to leave early in the spring is we must get a garden planted early as possible, we need to raise food to get us through that first winter. Turning sod for the first time makes very poor ground to plant a garden or anything in. Hopefully, we can find land near a creek where there should be some rich loose soil for a garden. There might still be land near that big lake where Torvald Johnson has his place, if that is the case, we will be close to the water which would be fine with me.

"We will have to carry water in any case until I dig a well. There is plenty of small game such as prairie chickens, the lakes all have fish. We might be living off the land literally, for a long time. There is no wood up on the prairie land, but I understand there are many lakes. Wood for cooking and heating will be gathered using driftwood or cut wood that has fallen by the lake shores. We will bring it home for the stove. It sounds like buffalo chips that have been dried in the hot sun are plentiful. Some people end up rolling tall grass together, then tie in knots, for fuel. We will need anything that burns to keep warm with and to cook. As I have told you, none of this will be easy.

"My cousin, Ole, is planning on returning to America in a year or two. His wife died giving birth to their fifth child. He came here three years ago with our cousin Torvald Johnson to look the Dakota Territory over thoroughly. Torvald chose some land near a large lake, it is several miles across and an excellent place for fishing, hunting, and trapping. Ole helped Torvald build a sod house to live in. When enough sod is turned, and the land is producing crops they will build a wood frame home right near that Lake then his family will arrive. While Ole was there, he made enough money trapping furs to pay for his trip back to Norway to get his family.

"The people moving to the lake area were mostly Norwegian and Finnish. Torvald built the first sauna near the lake. After working, turning sod all day, if you took a good hot sauna bath you could roll the dirt right off your body, it cleaned the pores out very good. A hot sauna bath made you feel all clean when you got done. Torvald's home became a meeting place on Saturday night. Everyone would either walk or arrive by horse and wagon, and in the wintertime horse and bobsled. Each family would bring something for lunch. Saturday night was spent visiting and taking a hot sauna. Some of the hardy ones jumped from the sauna into the cold lake water, an invigorating thing for sure. Most of the group coming to the sauna would have a church service there at his farm. They would later build a church and have a regular church service each week. Torvald and later Simon were both lay preachers and baptized many babies. The community was growing fast. Wagon trails were starting to be turned into more than paths. A road grader pulled by six or eight horses was used to make roads. Then ditches filled with snow, farmers made manure bridges to get on the road before driveways were made.

"A little town sprang up every six or eight miles wherever the railroad went because the steam locomotives needed to take on water many times as they traveled, and then there was coal stored at some towns where the train would fill up with coal again. It was mostly freight but it didn't take long and there were as many passenger trains as there were freight trains. Some trains got stuck in the deep snow. That created work for a lot of snow shovels to come to the rescue and get the train rolling again.

"Torvald wrote a letter home shortly after they had built the sod house; they were awakened one morning by the dog barking, so they looked out through the hole in the door. A half dozen young Indians were standing out in front of the soddy, looking the place over. Ole opened the door and bent down to go out. When he straightened up to his full height the Indians took one quick, wide-eyed look then quickly left, walking along the lake shore. Those young Indians must have gotten back to their village in a hurry and reported to everyone that a giant Norwegian just moved into the neighborhood. The Indians had a small village on the opposite side of the lake. You didn't see many canoes because there was no birch-bark to make them from. The lake is so large, the waves get extremely high during windstorms. You would need a seaworthy boat to ride those waves. I believe there will be great potential to catch and sell fish from there to other people. The nearest town is Volga, but there is a small store on the northwest side of the lake. We will have to go to it for basic supplies and I imagine they have some hardware and dry goods. The train hasn't got that far north, all merchandise has to go by rail to Volga and then delivered by ox team or horses and wagon up toward the Lake Country.

"My father heard the description of the place they had chosen, he wanted to move too. He then decided not to at his advanced age, he didn't think he was up to making the trip. Father was so excited over the prospect of the fishing, he went to work and made us a 50-foot gill net. That is our wedding present from my mother and father, so I know he cares about you, Anna. Mother made us a pillow out of that net, we will add lead weights when we get ready to use it. He also told me a tobacco can filled with Norway's best-assorted fishhooks, was placed in the center of the pillow, so we wouldn't have a lump to sleep on. My father takes pride in his net making, he used the finest grade of materials so it will last. We must guard that pillow very closely. It was mother's thinking if we lose everything, we will still have our pillow. It could aid in providing food to sustain us. We will catch fish with that net to eat, smoke and dry, salt brine in crocks and sell for money or trade for food at the store.

"I know cousin Ole will be a big help with the heavy work when he returns. We will need him, especially if we decide to build a stone house. I understand fieldstone is plentiful, they are good for building things but not worth much when you must pick them up to plant your crops. Cousin Ole was a forester and has been doing hard work ever since he was a teenager, he is a big, strong man now. Ole is the most soft-spoken, easy-going man you'll ever meet, but he has had to do a lot of fighting in his life. He is a foot taller than the average man and every place he went somebody who thought they were tough, bully-type guy, would pick a fight with him. Ole would just pick them up off the ground and shake them a little and turn them loose. They always had enough quickly, then left in a hurry. Somebody was stealing furs from his traps one time. Ole caught the guy, talked to him, told him it was wrong to steal then told him that he should leave that area. He got so scared that he left the country and moved to a different place. People suspected Ole of killing him. I know my cousin Ole could never kill anyone. He did scare the guy enough to make him change his ways with one sermon."

Louie was late getting home one night from work it was almost the middle of the night. Anna was worried and scared. Louie finally got home, as he walked into the house Anna could smell liquor. She said, "Louis, what have you done, I never thought you would go to that rowdy saloon and drink. Whatever made you do that?"

Louie said, "That is not what happened. We had a cave-in at the mine, the water was flooding the tunnel. I was never so scared in my life, we got the water to slow down and reopened the passage, so we could crawl out. None of us thought we would get out, but we crawled from that small hole like a bunch of drowned rats. I have never been so cold and miserable. My teeth were chattering so hard I thought they might break off. The shift foreman felt bad for our plight, he brought out a keg of brandy and told everybody to drink some and get their blood circulating again. I think he was celebrating the fact that we did not lose our lives down in the mine. Yes, Anna, we are bound to go to Dakota Territory. It will only be a few more months now."

She said, "Louie, I am so sorry for doubting you, please forgive me."

"There is nothing to forgive. I love you, Anna. I will have to send Torvald Johnson a letter before we leave here, telling him what day we will get to Volga on the train. He will meet us there with a wagon and team of horses. He said we could stay at his place until we get our homestead land chosen and get our home ready. We will need a small stove for cooking, and a few kitchen items that we don't have in the trunk. It will be a small operating budget to start with. The land is being grabbed up fast, so we want to be sure we get there early in the spring."

Chapter 3

Dakota Territory

They claimed their share of the promised land in Dakota Territory USA in March 1879. It had a sloping hillside near a big lake where they dug their future home. There was more than enough rock to work with for building a stone house later. The original dugout ended up being the root cellar too. A large part of the quarter section was a marsh, a slough or bog, with muskrat houses on it. That meant part of that land would be too wet to farm on most years, leaving fewer tillable acres. To help make up for that, there would be some income gained from selling muskrat hides to fur buyers. Anna immediately went to work planting a garden down by the edge of the marsh, there was rich soil and hopefully a garden would do well. The mosquitoes attacked her ferociously during hot weather. They luckily found a good used stove after someone had upgraded to a large cook stove. Anna was tired of cooking over an open fire, she was pleased to get the stove. It would work good for cooking and keeping the house warm, better than working with an open fire pit.

Anna was pregnant and they were both very happy. About midsummer, she had a miscarriage. Louie felt terrible and guilty, he became depressed thinking it was because she was working so hard in the garden. They were fortunate in acquiring a pair of oxen and some equipment from a farmer who was starting to use horses. The oxen were very dependable and could do well on the prairie grass, instead of feeding them higher quality hay. Louie hired a neighbor to break 10 acres of sod the first year, everything was done manually, planting, harvesting, all of it. The dugout home was quite snug and comfortable, it was made into the south side of a large hill, so the sun shone on it. They fashioned a window and door on that sunny south wall. Their new home was cool on the hot summer days and it was easy to heat in the wintertime which made them quite happy. An eight-foot wall of stone with cottonwood tree branches leaning against it, was a planned shelter for the oxen.

The Karlson family spent their first winter in their cozy dugout. Anna was very talented and turned a man-made cave into a comfortable one-room home. They had one very bad storm that first winter, it was a blinding blizzard and the temperature was almost 40 below zero. Louie didn't have the roof finished on the shelter for the oxen, so he brought the oxen into the dugout with them. They had real crowded conditions until the storm ended three days later. They did not want to repeat that very often. She had been busy all summer, growing things in the garden and preserving everything for storage to get them through the winter months. Chris was by her side all the time. They were very fortunate to have raised a couple 100 pounds (ca. 45 kg) of potatoes which should be plenty for them. They could trade some potatoes to neighbors for eggs. Carrots kept in a huge crock, beans were drying behind the stove. She grew different kinds of squash, they kept well in a hole dug further into the back wall. A shallow well was dug not far away from the marsh. It had very hard water in it but it was clean if you were careful filling your bucket. It was much better than dipping water from the slough or carrying it from the lake. The hard water was boiled for drinking. A small general store was three miles (4.83 kilometers) away, that was the only place they could get staple items or necessities for day-to-day living.

Louis was reflecting about their crossing one day on the steamship. He said, "Anna, those hoity-toity folks in first class wouldn't even say hello to me, good morning, or give me the time of day. I have to smile now that they are wearing my muskrat furs and probably think they have mink coats. I have thanked the Lord many times for putting Ingeborg Johansson on that ship. If she hadn't been there to help, I don't know what we would have done. If I had lost you, I would have jumped overboard."

Frances Olson & (Brother) Karlton going to town in 1935.

Frank Olson (My father) Cutting grain

Steam threshing Circa 1908

In the spring of 1881, Louie sent a letter to his cousin Ole.

1 April 1881
Dear Ole,

If you're coming to America you better hurry up, the land is being taken up fast. We would be happy if you would come and help build us a stone house. A hillside over by the lake slid down during high-water years. It exposed some excellent clay to use for mortar, it looks like a combination of clay and limestone. The land we homesteaded has about 40 acres of marsh on it, I have harvested enough muskrats to make up for the grain that we haven't been able to harvest. A neighbor plowed up another 10 acres of sod, and we planted wheat and corn, but we barely grew enough to keep our animals alive. The muskrat money has helped us buy some harvesting equipment, a milk cow and a few chickens. I'm going to start building a small barn, it will have stone walls, and we will buy wood to put on the roof. We hope to hear from you soon. Everything has been going well here, except Anna had a miscarriage. Our son Chris is growing up to be a young man, helping his mother with everything.

You will have to come and teach me how to trap mink. The dirty rascals eat my muskrats right out of the traps, just eating the heads and ruining the valuable part of the fur. I try to catch those smart mink but have very poor luck. I know you could catch them if you were here.

Love,
Cousin Louie, Anna, and Chris

"Anna, I wrote a letter to Ole and told him he better hurry and come over here before the land is all gone and that we would like to have him help us build a stone house. I know he is reluctant to leave his parents alone in Norway, but they won't be alone as there are three other sisters still living at home. I presume if they marry, their husbands will help their father on the farm. Ole did talk about bringing his four children and having his brother Simon come too. Simon and his wife have four daughters and no sons. Ole's son, Andrew, will help Simon with his farming operation.

When I told him about the income we made trapping muskrats, I'm sure that will light a fire under his tail feathers and get him moving faster. Ole loves to hunt and fish, and trapping he is very good at."

The hot summer of 1881 was a scorcher for the pioneers living in Dakota Territory USA. The wind blew hard, hot and dry all that summer, crops withered in the field. Thunderstorms developed almost daily but no rain came out of the troubled, unforgiving, reddish purple sky, only lightning. The electricity charged heavens sent bolts of deadly lightning, starting numerous prairie fires throughout the region. Many families who had wood frame houses, lost their homes and belongings to the destructive prairie fires. Some called them, "The Fires from Hell." The wind-driven flames traveled fast through the tall, dry prairie grass, burning everything in their path. There were several fires every day burning simultaneously throughout the territory. A suffering people were tested more with each passing day. Religious people were starting to lose their faith in a creator that would allow the destruction of that which he had created. They determined the fires must have come from hell.

Prairie Fires burned around this house

Ole and Simon with their families came from Norway in 1881, and they worked at the iron mines of Northern Minnesota where several cousins were working. They continued their journey west in 1883, against a strong urge to remain in Minnesota where there was steady work. The dream to seek farmland won over security. They arrived in Volga on the train and then purchased oxen and a wagon to make the trip north to the big lake.

Dakota Territory was entering a time of drought. The weather seemed to run in cycles of 10 years, if that was the case, a dry cycle started in 1881. Louie's muskrat revenue soon ended, there was no water in the marsh, the well, even, went dry, they now had to carry water for a mile from a neighbor's place. Daily life and their future looked very bleak, then Anna had another miscarriage. Ole and Simon arrived in the fall of 1883 and were very disappointed in what they found. They brought with them the news about new land being opened to homestead in North Dakota. It was just as rich farmland as that in South Dakota.

Ole, Simon, and Andrew immediately went to work helping Louie build a stone house. The hard work kept them in good spirits. They were all in agreement there had never been a stone house erected any faster than that one. And they had to haul clay and limestone for a mile from the east side of the lake. The oxen worked overtime, dragging large stones from the field to the building site. They needed some very large rocks for cornerstones. It was a major undertaking getting them loosened and out of the ground as they were usually buried with more than half of the rock underground. There were no large stones right in the vicinity where they wanted to build the house. They had to dig with shovels all around the rock, then using heavy iron crowbars pry and leverage them loose, then get them loaded on a stone boat they had made. The stone boat was made of heavy timbers from near the lake, heavy log chains were on one end to drag it with. After they got the stone dug loose enough, they rolled or slid it on to the stone boat then start dragging it toward the building, the oxen straining with every lurching tug of the way. They had to go through that same routine with about two dozen large rocks which was tiring out the oxen greatly. Smaller stones they would pile on the stone boat and bring them back several at a time. They had an old piece of canvas tarp to lay on the stone boat when they went after the clay and limestone. It was a very labor-intensive project, everyone ate heartily and slept the sleep of the exhausted every night. It was a cramped space to live in.

Andrew was planning to dig the well deeper, but they all decided to send him to the store three miles away. The general store had just had some new water pumps delivered.

Andrew took the horses and wagon to get a water pump with a four-inch cylinder making it capable of delivering a large quantity of water with little effort. He also bought a two-inch sand point, two five-foot sections of well pipe and a union, also a pounding cap. When he got back they used pipe wrenches and connected one pipe to the sand point, put the cap on the other end, then drove it into the ground, took the pounding cap off and connected the union and the second pipe, then capped it, pounded it into the ground until about two-feet were sticking out, then took off the cap. It was time to put the pump on, then build up a foundation with some rocks around it filled with mortar. After the pump was in place, Anna brought some priming water and poured it down into the pump. Andrew started to pump, nothing came. Andrew stopped pumping for a minute, Anna brought another bucket of water and slowly poured it in the top of the pump while Andrew pumped as fast as he could. Pretty soon the pump got harder to push down, Andrew said, "We've got water coming, I can feel it." He pumped more and out came a bunch of muddy water. Louie took over to give Andrew a break, he pumped the water for a long time until it ran clear.

They all shouted out in celebration, "We have water, we have water." It was a happy day, they finally had water that didn't have to be strained or boiled. It was nice and clean. Andrew told Louie, "Now you have a place for the turkeys to roost at night. There's an old saying, 'nothing is slicker than turkey poop on the pump handle,' and now you get to experience that. I believe that saying came from the old country."

Simon, his wife and children were going to spend the winter at Torvald Johnson's new house. They were content to work for room and board. Ole would stay there with the Karlsons.

After a long discussion, weighing the pros and cons, they arrived at the decision to make the move to North Dakota in the spring and claim land there. Four other families, mostly first and second cousins planned to go with them. It was decided: Ole, Louie, Anna, and Chris would go to North Dakota and the others would stay there in the stone house. Andrew was returning to Minnesota to work for another year, maybe two. Ole's youngest son Olaf died shortly after getting off the ship, his other two children would live with childless couples looking for someone to work for room and board. Etta moved in with a nearby couple who had no children. Gideon started living with the family who owned the store on the north side of the lake.

It wasn't long before Gideon was making regular trips, hauling wheat to a grinding mill on the Big Sioux River 60 miles (ca. 97 km) away. He was only 17 years old, a young teamster with a big responsibility. For someone his age to take off with an oxteam and a wagon loaded with wheat, made his father proud. It was ground into flour to bring back for the people to survive the long winter on. Gideon was a brave, young man to travel past Sioux Indian villages along the Big Sioux River. He became good friends with many of them because he would bring them tobacco.

There were no roads at that time and few wagon trails between the two or three communities that had just started to grow. The prairie grass was tall, if you traveled very close to the river you would get stuck in mud where runoff rainwater ran towards the river. He had to avoid those boggy places, getting stuck meant unloading the wagon, pulling it from the mud, then reloading it. Gideon made several trips before he had himself a route mapped out where he could make the best time. When he first started out, it took him about 10 days to make the trip. After he had been doing it for a couple years, he was getting the time traveled down to eight days each way. Many of the settlers living around the lake didn't use tobacco, but they were very grateful to Gideon taking the risk going after flour. They generously supported his tobacco fund, it created a safe passage for him to get the flour. The Indians welcomed Gideon with open arms when they would see him coming. He was a good trapper and hunter himself and when he camped on the prairie, he would build a fire and roast a prairie chicken, or eat fresh fish if he was close to the river. He had a frying pan, coffee pot, and a good supply of hardtack instead of bread. His family always enjoyed hardtack made from rye flour. Hardtack was a very good, lightweight food item to carry with you traveling by ship, horseback, foot, or wagon train. It was so dry it would never spoil, it was a very healthy food for survival. The hardtack they had in the old country, was thin, about 10 inches in diameter with a two-inch hole in the center. A large quantity of the crunchy treat could be stored on a wooden pole and hung in the rafters of the cabin, taking up little space.

He also had a supply of dried, or smoked fish in his wagon, and buffalo jerky next to his water canteens. Gideon got along with the Indians from the start because he was about the most soft-spoken, quietest man ever to come out of Norway. He never raised his voice or said a bad word in his life. Not even to an ox. He lived to be 94 years old.

When he got married in his twenties, a lot of people were building wood frame homes on the prairie. Gideon became a professional lath and plaster man, also cistern designer. He went into business with his sister's husband Ole Johnston. They became famous for finishing walls with horsehair plaster, in hundreds of new homes being built on the prairie. They also built cisterns to catch rainwater running off roofs, some held thousands of gallons of water. Many of the cisterns measured 14 feet deep and eight-foot wide. Some people hung jars of milk down in the cistern to keep it cool. People living in sod houses often dug deep postholes, then hung milk or yogurt down the holes to keep it cool. After the cistern and plastering jobs started to slow down, Gideon and Ole Johnston went in the stucco business. They put their famous stucco coating over the outside walls of wood frame homes, that cement overcoat would almost last for an eternity.

The first settlers coming to the Dakota Territory lived in dugouts in the side of a hill or made sod houses called a soddy from pieces of sod cut with a plow. The prairie families usually had a large number of children for the simple reason, all the work that had to be done was manual work. There were no machines for any of it. Even cutting grain and hay was done with a hand and arm operated scythe, then gathered with forks. The virgin sod had to be broken up, which was a slow, back-breaking process with oxen pulling a single-bottom plow or with horses. The family size grew as the acres of plowed land increased. A lot of farmers owned a section of land and then put their home and barns at the center of the section. That was a practical way of doing it, then they farmed out in four different directions from the center. Most of those families lived in a one-room frame house after they got out of the sod houses. Those one-room homes usually had a loft where the children slept. It had to be crowded, but it helped them keep warm in the wintertime. The size of homes grew as the amount of land being plowed increased. Two-story homes became common, some families with 15 children had three-story homes. The wood came in after the railroads arrived, building materials were available but expensive. Those farming a section of land, started to make money and that was multiplied thousands fold and a great nation grew from all that hardship, labor, and sweat.

Gideon and Ole Johnston's plaster and stucco business was a great success for them, they had all the work they could do within easy traveling distance. They were working on a three-story home one day, putting up stucco at the very peak of a roof when Ole fell from the tall ladder and broke his back. There were no doctors or hospitals at that time. Ole Johnston spent the rest of his life in an old wooden wheelchair starting in his 30s. Ole Johnston and Ettaborg (Gideon and Andrews sister) had a boy and a girl as did Gideon and Sophie. Ole often said they were too tired from working so hard to have more children than that.

He was a no-nonsense type of man and used some very colorful adjectives at times to get his point across, so he claimed. Ole had one of the first battery radios and never missed a news broadcast. He usually would say thank you as he quickly turned the radio off with a click, to save the battery. Ole Johnston read everything he could get his hands on and had all the newspapers in the area delivered to his house. He read every inch of each paper, editors of those papers and magazines got to know him well. If he read something that he didn't agree with he got out his pencil and paper to send a quick rebuttal. Politics was a sore spot with him, he didn't think any politician played by the rules. Not the rules they should go by such as the golden rule. He never claimed to have a religious side to him but visiting with him you soon saw a strong faith. Crippled as he was, he did not rely on his wife or children for help. Ettaborg did the cooking and housekeeping but Ole transferred himself from his wheelchair to his bed and to the toilet. He had a special commode by the bed he could transfer to and kept himself clean. He was a very proud independent person who lived to be almost 90 years old. How he kept from getting pressure sores is a miracle.

Andrew returned from Northern Minnesota where he worked in the iron mines for a few more years. That is where he met his wife Minnie, they had a daughter named Alice, then moved back to Dakota Territory. They rented land next to Simon and helped Simon farm for the rest of his life.

Andrew and Minnie, with help from neighbors, built a sod house half a mile from Simon's stone house. They lived in that soddy for many years until they accumulated enough cash to enclose it with a wood frame. They built the wood right around the original sod walls. It resembled a fortress with walls three-feet thick. They had two more children Frank (my father) and Elma and lived there for forty years. Their retirement years were spent on a farm two miles away. Mini came from Lapland with her family and settled in

Northern Minnesota where all the family members worked in the iron mines. Minnie loved her 'Sámi' family roots as reindeer herders and was very proud of her heritage. She continued to make various dishes using blood, they could not get blood of reindeer. At butchering time, beef blood was used instead of reindeer. Minnie told about men eating warm reindeer liver when they killed one. In the freezing cold of the Arctic Circle that would be quite a treat.

They loved what they called viili, (yogurt) made with a starter that was put into skim milk. It turned thick, you could almost chew it off when you took a drink of it out of a glass. If she ran low on starter, a letter got sent to people back in Finland. They would send her a piece of dishtowel that had been soaked in that special, craved starter. When Minnie got a letter back, she would open it and put a piece of that cloth in skim milk. It would only take a few days and they had viili again. It must have been equivalent to unflavored yogurt and been good for the digestive system. When they moved to their second farm there was no well for water, or refrigeration so they dug a well by hand and put on a hand-pump. It supplied hard water and plenty of it. The water ran through a wooden cooler to the cattle and horse tank, it kept their milk cool. In earlier years when they first moved to that land, they dug deep postholes in the ground and lowered the milk down on a string and it hung there during the day to stay cool for the evening meal. Andrew always had a crock jug from the Red Wing MN pottery factory. He wrapped a water-soaked burlap bag around that jug and filled it with water to take out in the field. He had cool drinking water from it most of the day.

Andrew and Minnie always raised many chickens. They would butcher some for eating but kept many laying hens for eggs to sell or trade for groceries at the store. They also milked a few cows and separated the cream from the milk, then sold the cream at the produce house near the railroad tracks, where buyers bought milk, cream, butter, eggs, and live chickens. Minnie always raised a huge garden, every vegetable and flower imaginable. It was hard to keep much on hand before the mason jar became available. She canned everything, including beef when they butchered. That mason jar with the rubber ring and zinc lid was an important part of history. A boiling canner on a hot cookstove in the heat of summer would be enough to test the strongest woman. Minnie did her canning in a summer kitchen on a kerosene stove. It was a major undertaking, beef had to be boiled for several hours to make it safe from botulism. They didn't can the fish, they salted them and kept them in a crock, such as she did pickles in a crock, then in later years fruit jars. There was a huge 30-gallon crock, they did salted pork or made beef brisket in. Before the jar came along carrots were kept in a large crock filled with sand. All of this became possible after they dug their first basement, and that was dug with horses pulling a handheld dirt scraper blade, and with men and shovels. Minnie wanted to get her chickens started early in the spring. She always bought Rhode Island reds, the baby chicks would come on the railroad at a certain day. They had to be there to pick them up and keep them warm. She started the chicks in the basement under a kerosene brooder, those little peepers were nice and warm. As soon as the weather permitted, she brought them outdoors into a sunny located brooder house.

Minnie always won many ribbons at the County and State Fair with her chickens. She loved those big Rhode Island Reds.

Things were looking great on the prairie when each family finally had their own outhouse. A lot of outside toilets had more than two holes as the families grew and more children were needing to use the toilet. A smaller seat or bench was put in for the kids to use. A two-hole was average, there was a small-town dentist who had a one-hole toilet right outside his back door. Every household had a chamber pot underneath the bed or in the closet, some were quite ornate. As a rule, the children used the pot in the house and then mom or dad would carry it out and dump it in the toilet. A lot of times if grandma or grandpa was living upstairs, as the second generation was downstairs, grandpa might lower the pot out of an upstairs window instead of carrying it through the house. He would then take it and dump it in the outhouse hole. The old outhouse became a great place to daydream, if the weather was nice. Winter trips were done in haste. Weather permitting, you might contemplate world travels, life ambitions, or sit and read a good book.

A special 'free' book became very popular in every outhouse on the prairie. It was the Montgomery Ward catalog. It was not a very popular book with local merchants in the little towns that were now being started. The general stores and small-town hardware that were springing up, looked at the catalogue from Montgomery Ward with deep, dark disdain. They would rather see the mail-delivery man lose his mailbags filled with catalogs. Montgomery Ward could sell items much cheaper. The local merchants cost had to include shipping by railroad, most felt it was very unfair. Some tried to have legislation passed to stop wards from infringing on their businesses, but no lawmakers were about to take on that task. They had bigger fish to fry. Children and adults read that catalog and dreamed of having the different items that were listed, for the ladies the latest women's fashions, toys for the kids, farming equipment, sporting equipment for the outdoors types. Mechanic tools for those handy at repairing things. It became known as the wish-book and people would sit there using the toilet facilities and wishing they had all the various items that they had been looking at. The index pages were softer paper, they were not glossy as the advertising pages were, the index pages soon disappeared from the catalog when it arrived in the outhouse. It was simply that much better wiping paper, toilet paper was a luxury, times were hard. It was too expensive to be used. Newspaper print worked if you wrinkled it in your hands a while, but still not soft and gentle. Some joked about using corncobs, if they came up clean you knew you were OK.

A lot of single men came from the Scandinavian countries mostly seeking any kind of work they could get, many remained bachelors. My grandparents had one older man working for them. One day, while he was dragging freshly turned sod with the horses and a drag, something happened that spooked the horses while he was cleaning weeds from the drag. Those horses started running and his overalls got caught on the harrow. He was dragged half a mile to the other end of the field, the poor man was all beat up and battered. There were no hospitals at that time and very few doctors. My grandmother took care of him, and nursed him back to health. He recovered but was never the same after that.

An aunt and uncle of mine had a hired man once, who was a confirmed bachelor. He was a hardworking, dedicated hired man, who worked for very few dollars a day, room and board and some chewing tobacco. He did not want his overalls washed, when they got dirty and a little stinky, he would put them in a burlap bag and hang them up in the haymow. After a week or so of letting them air out, he would take the sack down and change clothes putting the recent dirty ones in the bag. One day my aunt took his clothing bag down and washed everything in her machine, then dried them and hung the sack back up in the haymow. The old man was very agitated, "I told you I did not want those clothes washed." I guess it was his impression it wore out the fabric and they wouldn't last as long.

Another family had a hired man; for $4.00 a day, he would pitch manure out of a barn that had cattle in it all winter, the manure might be three-feet deep. He would go in there with a pitchfork and spend the whole day, every day. He had a break while the manure spreader was in the field. Two teams of horses and two spreaders, he didn't care, he pitched at the same speed all day long, like an automated pitchfork.

One couple had a hired man who was dragging the freshly turned sod. He was cleaning the drag section teeth, because they were full of weeds and grass. While he was holding one section up, his hand slipped and he dropped it, one sharp steel tooth went through his shoe and foot. He commented one time, "I knew there was no doctors around here," he said, "what else could I do, I took my shoe off and

40

peed on my foot, put my shoe back on and went to work again, I never even got infection in that foot."

Chapter 4

Off to North Dakota

It was a chilly, windy day in late March when the Olson Karlson group with all their belongings in two wagons pulled by two teams of oxen, started out for North Dakota. Severe snowstorms could come up at any time, temperatures might easily get down to freezing. They had their little stove in the back of one extra, sturdy wagon with some firewood. If the weather went sour on them and it got too cold to travel onward, they would crawl into the wagon and bundle up with their bedding to keep warm until the foul weather passed.

They joined four other families near the border, and all proceeded to an area near a small lake, it was later known as Duck Lake. Ole Olson and Louie Karlson claimed land that bordered the lake. To Ole's utter joy and amazement, it was filled with muskrat houses from the year before. It looked like no one ever trapped there. In his eyes, someone had left a gold mine unguarded and untouched. It was far too late for trapping at that time of year because the fur was not prime and had no value. Ole said to Louie, "Looking at this lake and the previous water levels, it is on its way down. You and I are going to have a very busy winter. We will have to trap muskrats around the clock, I'm sure this lake will be dry next year. I now wonder if we made a mistake by coming here, it appears there is a drought started that will continue up through the center of the continent. We are going to have to work hard this winter and do as much trapping as we can and save our money. I do not think we're going to grow many crops under the continuing dry conditions. We all know the Lord works in mysterious ways, but this is amazing! The mother muskrats living on this lake will have baby muskrats this summer, this is like money in the bank, drawing interest, it also could be how we will survive." Ole had good luck trapping mink, enough mink money was set aside so everyone could have a good Christmas. They also sold hides from coyote, fox, and badger. The pelts had a high value while longhaired fur coats remained in style. Buffalo hides got made into robes to put over your legs while riding on bobsled or wagon in cold weather. Large meals kept the hunger in check. At first, while living in North Dakota, the food consisted mainly of buffalo, prairie chicken, waterfowl, fish and muskrat meat. Muskrat meat is very rich and tasty but like anything else, the taste buds can only enjoy so much of it before rebellious reflux begins.

One of the first things that they had to do when they arrived at Duck Lake was to make a trip to the general store, which later became the town of Ryder. They purchased a sand point, a five-foot section of water pipe, and a hand-operated water pump. The location of their well was going to be right near the lake so one five-foot section of pipe was plenty to get down below the water level. They screwed a section of pipe onto the sand point and pounded it down into the ground until the pipe was just sticking out, then attached the water pump to it. Someone brought water from the lake and they primed the pump and had running water. All you had to do was pump it by hand. On many areas of the prairie water was much deeper, some places 100 or 200 feet. Wells like that had to be drilled with special equipment that cost a lot of money. Many areas on the prairie had water at 10 or 20 feet. People always tried to dig a well by hand so they could drop down a bucket. They would dig and get to eight feet and not find water so they would dig it down to 10 feet or 15 feet, and then the sides would cave in on them and they got buried alive. Many pioneer families lost loved ones who were just digging a well. Water was a precious thing.

That land was flat as pee on a plate, no hillside for a dugout house, the first thing they had to do was start cutting sod for building material to build a house with. They slept in the wagons or out under the stars for a couple of weeks. There were numerous cottonwood trees around the lake; many had fallen from the ice on the lake, pushing them over or from windstorms. They didn't have to cut many, it was mostly just gathering up large branches that were already on the ground, it made their task much easier. Tree branches got put across the top of the walls and then sod up on the tree branches. The grass would start growing, and they would have a grassy roof that would shed water to some degree. After getting their soddy finished, they went to work, breaking more ground then dragging it to plant some wheat and corn. Their spirits and hope got low, while good planting seed into powder dry ground. The chance of it growing was small. They had to pray for rain or maybe talk to some local Indians and request a rain dance.

In 1884, the people farming near Duck Lake harvested a meager crop. It yielded barely enough income to pay for the seed and the animals to survive on. That strong-willed groups' desperate situation became magnified many times over in 1885 when influenza broke out. That dreaded virus claimed nearly half of those recent arrivals. Grieving and sadness was the order of the day, the men were exhausted from digging graves. A spot, half a mile away, had a small rise overlooking the lake. After a short meeting, it became unanimous that it was the perfect location to create a Pioneer Cemetery. That was the end of the trail, the final resting place for many relatives in that group. Their dreams had been dashed by a devil disease, spirits got trodden-on and tested. Many knew, down deep, they must carry on, some alone, better days would come. Faith and hope must prevail.

Anna gave birth to a big baby girl in the fall of 1885, they named her Mary. That baby was healthy and Anna and Louie were proud, thankful parents for the second time. The mother and baby both faced the influenza virus and won.

In 1886, Duck Lake became shallow enough to walk across, that was the beginning of the end for the trapping bonanza, not much muskrat income to rely on. It was so dry, only thistles grew. The tumbleweeds blew around as if they were assorted demons escaping the fires of hell on that parched land. Constantly blowing hot winds, howled day and night, nothing but dust storms. Flying dust blew around as if it was powdery snow, it drifted over the fences. Dust found the way through the smallest cracks, around doors and windows, filtering into the houses, covering the kitchen table with dirt. A dishtowel was commonly used to cover up the sugar bowl and other items. Some wore a handkerchief over their faces, so they didn't breathe in the talcum dry dust.

Food for survival became a problem for everyone. The jackrabbits in the area and cottontails became scarce, most of the waterfowl had flown south for the winter. They had not been able to raise any beef or pork and only a few chickens to supply them with meat. A big part of their protein was muskrat meat and now that was about gone too. Some of the men who were bored with being trapped inside of the soddy all winter, devised ways to catch the snow birds. There always was a lot of snowbirds flying in the wind and drifting snow, they would scratch around in the snow near the sod houses. It was food that had to be captured, different ways of catching those little birds was devised such as snaring. The tiny birds tasted very good for a change of pace food.

A large area on Duck Lake was filled with cattails, that became a part of everyone's diet. Just about every part of the cattail could be used in one way or the other. The white root was eaten almost like potatoes or yams in fall and winter. They were high in starch and very nutritious. Early in the spring while the tops of the cattails were still green, with a lot of imagination, they could be eaten like corn on the cob. The people gave thanks daily, fortunate to have those cattails in the lake. It was more than a single harvest. As seasons changed, different parts of the plant could be used. From early in the spring until late fall, they were in competition with the muskrats. The muskrats made their winter homes with large piles of cattail they cut off with their sharp teeth. They dug up the roots, then stored them in piles for the winter months. The muskrats survived the long cold winters by eating the roots of the cattails. Many of the Karlson women spent hours scraping and drying the cattail roots, then pounding them to make flour, because they had no wheat or rye flour left. Those roots made a very nutritious flour for cooking. The cattail pollen which was plentiful in the late fall after the plants became dormant, made an excellent flour for cooking, it just took some getting used to. It was much different from wheat and rye flour. In the spring, they ate new shoots on the cattail stalks as if it was asparagus. The muskrats were mostly gone but the cattails remained.

The tall lush prairie grass dried up during the hot summer forcing the buffaloes farther west toward the Missouri River. That ended the fresh meat supply for everyone in the area. The women and children accumulated firewood around the lake most of the year and piled it around the soddy. The woodpile was almost as big as the house, so it would last them through the winter. A depleting firewood supply prompted the picking up of buffalo chips, that became a daily chore, harvesting dried buffalo chips off the windswept prairie. The buffaloes were gone but the evidence of all the grass they consumed made good fuel for the stoves. The driftwood around the lake was buried under snow now, that was why they stockpiled so much during the good weather.

The Karlson group knew they were facing some very serious conditions, a decision had to be made. Duck Lake's hardy residents' faith was tested again as they shivered through that cold windy winter, cuddled up together trying to keep warm. Most of the winter their stomachs talked to them. There was no good Christmas that year.

The water in Duck Lake nearly dried-up and the winter snow covering the ice kept the sun from shining through, consequently, the fish died of lack of oxygen in the shallow water. The smell of decaying, rotten fish lingered into the warm summer days. There was really nothing for those folks to stay there for now, the move was a mandatory thing at this point.

Ole Olson said to his cousin Louie Karlson, "We better pack up our wagons again, while we still have some money. The way I see it, the foothills of the Rocky Mountains up in Alberta Canada is our last hope. It is just now being opened to homesteaders. We will have to learn to get along with the Black Foot and a couple other tribes of Indians still living there, but there is land to be claimed. That is truly the last frontier as far as homesteading property goes, and from what I understand it is very desirable land. We will have to clear a certain amount of timber from it every year before we can farm it. You know me, I will be right at home in the forest, making the wood chips fly off my double-edged ax. What do you say, Louie? You better talk it over with Anna, you now have another child."

"I'm sure we will all be healthy and happy in that environment, the winters are cold and long, usually much snow, but it is a great land. The land up there is identical to what we left back in Norway, we will feel like we're back home again, that is worth much. It has a very short growing season, we were born near the Arctic Circle, we know not many fruit trees will grow there."

One of the families decided to stay at Duck Lake, on the land that came at such a terrible price. The manager of the little general store was happy to give them credit, so they would stay. Their money was depleted but not their faith and the manager of that small store on the prairie also had faith and a good heart, trusting the people.

Chapter 5

Destination: Alberta, Canada

In late March 1887, they left Duck Lake. Ole was driving one team of oxen and wagon, Louie was driving the other team with the second wagon. They were traveling close together, and they soon learned the oxen seemed to work better if Ole was on one side walking, while Louie walked in front of his team.

Two other families joined them. The little wagon train was on the move again, they truly hoped it would be the promised land this time. Anna, Chris, and baby Mary were bundled up in the back of one wagon amongst their quilts and furnishings. They had packed everything they owned again, and were headed for the Rocky Mountains. They could still be caught in some bad weather in March at Alberta, but again they had a little stove and firewood in the wagon.

They were surprised as they were crossing Saskatchewan, it had very good wagon trails. They had been heavily traveled by pioneers seeking new land. The wind was blowing as it did nearly daily, the oxen had a lot of fresh air going straight into their noses. A local farmer told them about gophers, some days gophers must hang on to the sides of the hole because if they let go the wind will blow them away. That is why you always see a gopher stick only his nose out at first, he's testing to see what kind of wind is blowing. Ole and Louie found many people turning sod, it also was rich farmland. Enough people had already moved to that area. They passed a small pioneer cemetery. It had several dozen graves in it, a harbinger what to expect if you're going to seek your fortune turning sod on the lone prairie. The buffalo grass didn't look as tall in Saskatchewan as it was in the Dakotas, there were still a few buffaloes in the area.

Ole said, "Louie, after leaving Black Deer and starting West, we have about 48 miles (ca. 77 km) of tough sledding, I mean travel, the snow should be melted by now. They get welcome, warm air flows off the ocean; it can build your spirits immensely after a long cold winter, but we hope the winter snows have melted by now in the foothills. We are going to an area where the Hudson Bay Company had a fur trading post almost 100 years ago. It was situated where the Clearwater and North Saskatchewan rivers come together. If we can get land there, I believe it's going to be one of the best places, we both like to hunt, fish and trap. We should feel right at home there.

"Louie, when I was helping Torvald Johnson build his sod house we had a visitor one time traveling through." He was a friendly little Frenchman, a trapper who had spent a lot of time in Canada. This fellow talked like he spent a few years in that area around the Rocky Mountain House fur trading post, and he worked a trap line in several directions from Rocky. It sounded as if there were some trails going east from there along the waterway toward Sylvan Lake, but it was tough going, that would be the trail we want. He was traveling through Dakota Territory going to Minnesota, but I recall him saying something about a map was made by the fur traders and it showed a very old mining trail between Black Deer and a little lake called Sylvan Lake. I don't know how I got to talking to him about it, at that time we had no idea of ever going there. He described a good picture of it to me because he spent a lot of time there. Sylvan Lake sounds like it's about midway between Black Deer and our destination where the rivers come together, and the fur-trading fort is located. We will stay on that trail as long as we can there is a river or waterway of some type coming down from the mountains to feed Sylvan Lake. We will have to just travel along as best we can and follow that water way. Hopefully the water will be low but that is doubtful at this time of the year. With all the snow melting it's probably running with a lot of rapids in it. We don't want to try crossing it, we need to stay on the south side of that water. We're going to have to spend a lot of time praying about it, God willing we will end up at the foothills of Rockies where the rivers come together.

It was their plan to arrive at Black Deer as early as possible. There was a wagon trail all the way across Southern Canada going straight north to Black Deer, from west there was no trail, you have to make one as you go west. Westbound travelers knew they would be following the path of the least resistance. If you had to clear a tree for your wagon to get through you surely did not want to cut a big one. It was best to have someone in the group walking, scouting the area further ahead, but still within shouting distance. They knew it was going to be painfully slow going. Few people had ventured west from that point by wagon, it was mostly uninhabited since the early fur traders came through. They found a lot of mud, spending extra time getting the wagons unstuck from deep mud, it exhausted the oxen to a point of worry and concern about getting to their destination.

Each day, they reflected on the coming winter and survival basics. A long hard back and sore muscle summer was approaching, all work, and absolutely no play. They had to get a cabin built, dig a well, start a garden, and get firewood cut for the winter. There would be much to do and a short time to do it in. To the average person it would seem impossible. As soon as they got their wagons unloaded, a small area was cleared and a garden planted. They made a shelter with the canvas around the wagon boxes, that was their home to start with.

The plan was to cut trees off a couple acres first, to build a one-room cabin. They would quickly clear the brush and plow it, then plant some wheat and oats for hay and grain to feed the animals. Louie and Ole had good sharp tools and they had the equipment to keep them sharp. They had a new five-foot long, two-man saw for cutting down the larger trees, and three buck saws for cutting off the limbs. There were three different axes and a few splitting wedges they could use for notching the wood for the cabin. They went to work on the large trees with the two-man saw, cutting down a couple dozen trees. Then, they all went to work with bucksaws cutting off the branches. Chris even had a smaller saw and did a lot of work cutting branches off. As a log was prepared it would be dragged to the building site, notched, then put in place. It became a routine that just kept going, one log after the other until the cabin was built. The stump removal became a major problem, but they had to get the stumps out so they could plant a little wheat and oats for the animals. They each had a shovel, Chris was helping too, to dig the dirt away so the roots could be cut. It was hard digging into the ground with the roots there, then cut them off with an axe or a small pruning saw. They would dig around the roots just enough to be able to cut them off, then hook a chain on the stump and have the oxen drag the stump right out. It was just a matter of a few days and they had a large pile of stumps and small branches. Some of the branches that they cut off the trees could be used for firewood later in the winter. They were making good progress, after they had an acre cleared, they hurried and plowed and dragged it, then planted wheat and oats. All this time Anna was planting a garden on the first little spot that they cleared, and she had baby Mary out there with her so she could keep an eye on her. The mud that almost drove them mad as they were traveling was now their friend in a way. A lot of the ground was muddy enough so they could pull smaller trees out with a heavy long chain and both ox teams pulling together. Pulling them out of the ground, roots and all, saved them days of hard work, creating a mood of celebration that they were not expecting. Ole announced over dinner the day they pulled the first tree roots and all, "The Lord had a hand in this clearing operation, we all must admit that."

The place where they settled was about five miles from the big general store and fur trading post at Rocky. It had been in business almost a hundred years, ever since the first fur traders and explorers came through the country seeking a passage over the mountains. The supplies to keep the fort and trading post running, all came up the river by boat. They were isolated in the winter months when boat traffic stopped because of ice. Plans on what to buy had to be made well in advance, the trading post had almost anything people needed. Making that trip could be a daunting, dangerous task in the wrong weather.

While they were building their new home, a big Saint Bernard dog showed up, he decided he was going to live there too, and he became their dog, King. Dog and boy, both had happy outgoing dispositions. King and Chris were best friends from day one, it was as if they had known each other all their lives.

Ole Olson and the Karlsons had been living in Alberta for nearly four years and were settled in, well and happy. Despite what they had been through since leaving Norway, they were all in good health and very fit. Their plans were to spend the rest of their lives in the foothills of the Canadian Rockies. There was not a better place anywhere on this earth unless it was where they grew up in Norway as children.

They had many cousins in several different families. First and second cousins from the same area in Norway, had settled around this area at Rocky. Ole had another brother Eston with a large family move there. It was hard to get together with people because you had to travel on foot or horseback, there were still no roads. Hopefully, the trails would keep improving until they resembled roads.

Ole and Louie were busy hunting, fishing or trapping when they were not clearing land to farm. The homestead law required them to clear a set number of acres of land each year to take out the timber. They had plenty of logs, and were now living in a two-room, log house. Ole helped other cousins moving into the area too. There had been enough homesteaders moving into the area, a school district was started. A cousin of theirs, Felix Olson, donated the land for the school to be built on and land for a cemetery. There were 12 children in that family, all very happy to have a school to go to. The schoolhouse was about two miles (3.22 kilometers) from where they lived, centrally located for the major population. Chris didn't think too much of the idea, but he did go to school, he was a very good student. There were still no roads, during a wet spring travel could become impossible. The land was so swampy, roads of logs were built in some areas, corduroy roads were the only way across some areas of swamp. A bridge was impractical because of cost and no way to anchor it.

Travel by wagon or bobsled was a luxury, traveling on foot, snowshoes, or skis was how people got to their destination. The speed of the travel was regulated by the weather. If there was not much snow, travel was by wagon or bobsleds. If the snow was soft and deep, you may have had to use skis or snowshoes. If it was rainy, spring weather, it was usually too muddy to go anywhere. Travel was simply slogged along walking, that was the easiest way to go from place to place. Winter temperatures could be life threatening.

Chapter 6

Ole Killed by Grizzly Bear

Ole went up on the mountain to his favorite hunting spot, King went with him. The dog always went hunting with him when Chris was at school. It was a warm fall afternoon, almost too nice for hunting deer, but Ole felt they should have more meat in the smokehouse in case the snow got too deep to do any hunting during the winter. The good life, sitting by a deer trail in the warm afternoon sun and taking a nap, the warm sun on his face. He thought to himself, *It won't be warm much longer, not to lay here like this. Soon, it will be snow and wind, with freezing cold weather.* They will be confined to living close to the cabin, bringing in firewood, checking the smokehouse, making sure things were not frozen in the root cellar. He was dreaming about his wife who died in Norway, he had a vison, a clear picture of his wife, Ingebor, in his mind when they were young. She was the tallest girl in the community and he was the tallest boy. He continued growing until he was 6 feet and 10 inches tall. They became passionately and deeply in love, soon after they met. They had five children, first came Gideon Joas, then little Etta (Ingeborg Jetta). Etta remained tiny her whole life, she was a petite young lady. A couple of years later Christian Andreas (Andrew my grandpa) was born. The fourth child was Ole Vilhelm (Olaf). Ole died just before he turned three, shortly after they landed in America. He missed his mother so badly he lost the will to live. Ingebor died during childbirth with their fifth child (unnamed).

Ole's loving memories of his wife ended abruptly when he heard a deep growl come from King, who was laying right beside him. The big dog growled again, before Ole could react a huge bear grabbed him by the left leg. That big brute was dragging him away, he hung on tight to his gun. King ran over and tried to bite the bear, it swatted King as if he was a fly. King got tossed through the air, it looked like he was dead when he hit the ground. Ole was in a panic, knowing that the bear was going to kill him and eat him. He tried to hold on to his gun and shoot the bear through the heart and lungs, so it would die quick. The bear refused to give him a clean shot at his front or his side, the bear was starting to run, dragging Ole. He shot his rifle as fast as he could at the side of the bear's head. It let out a loud growl then spit his leg out. The bear acted like it was going to leave, then turned around and grabbed Ole by the head, feeling the creature's hot breath, he was about to meet his maker. The bear spit Ole's head out, then spun around and started chewing on his left leg again. He was still conscious as the bear was tearing the flesh off his leg, he could hear the bones crunching in his leg, and feel the blood flowing as he passed out. The last thing that went through Ole's mind was that he was back in Norway, just a boy and was supposed to be watching the milk cow. A bear chased him away and then killed their only milk cow.

When Ole didn't come home from hunting, they were all worried, and scared knowing something had happened to him. Ole was always careful, he was a good woodsman, not about to have an accident of any kind. It was many hours since sun down when they heard King outside. Anna opened the door, King was standing there with Ole's coat in his mouth, it was drenched, covered with his blood. Louie said, "Oh, my, I don't like the looks of this, not at all."

It looked as if King's hip was broken and all bloody, the dog slept by the stove, he whimpered and cried all night. In the morning, King could walk better but was limping badly. Louie didn't want to take the dog along when he and Chris went to look for Ole, but the dog insisted on going. That faithful old dog limped along beside them, you could see he was in a lot of pain as they went up the Mountain to Ole's hunting spot. There was Ole, a grizzly bear had killed him and eaten his legs off, then buried his remains part way in the ground. That bear was planning to come back and finish him when it got hungry again. They had a terrible, slow, heart-breaking trek walking back home, the dog beside them. King acted like he was mourning the loss of Ole too. Louie was thinking, *I have never seen a bear leave a track that big, almost double the average big bear. I'll bet Ole emptied his gun into that gigantic monster and it still wouldn't stop.*

Louie and Chris got back to the cabin, Anna was waiting, she looked as if she had been crying when the door opened. "What happened?"

"He was killed by a big grizzly bear, we buried him up there on his beloved mountain. He will have eternal rest there, just as if he had never left Norway."

Winter was long, sad, and lonely without Ole being there with his good-natured ways and sense of humor. Anna and Louie were sitting by the fire, she said, "Louie, it will never be the same here without Ole. Do you think we should stay, or should we leave this place?"

"We have our home here now, Anna, we're not getting any younger. Chris is doing good in school, he has a great future, soon Mary will be in school. I suppose we better stay right here where we're at. Hopefully, our future together here at the foothills of this mountain will keep getting better, and we will have some peace in our old age.

"As we sit here reminiscing, Anna, I know the Lord has been good to us. We have had many trials along the way, I'm afraid I don't have another move left in me. We have no choice but to stay here. I believe we will be OK, as Chris gets older, he can carry more of the load, doing firewood and hunting and all the other things required to stay in the country. Who knows, maybe when we get old we can move into Rocky, Chris and his family can live out here. Towns are starting and growing here just like they were out in Dakota Territory. As the railroad comes through, they need towns so another one is born. Every so many miles along the railroad track, we both know that will happen here in the Rocky Mountains also. Someday there will be a large town within a few miles of here. I know we must continue to trust in the Lord, he will guide us and take care of us no matter what happens. We have been very blessed."

As usual, the hunting season was good, there was plenty of meat in the smokehouse, another winter was soon coming to an end. They still had plenty to eat in their root cellar. They had potatoes, rutabagas, turnips, different kinds of squash for baking, onions, and carrots, and pickles in stone crocks. It had been a bountiful full year for them, they felt truly blessed, but now Ole was not there to share in their good fortune.

March was coming in like a lamb, weather was unusually warm and nice, even this far north. Shortly after noon one day, during that first week, a strong storm came from the northwest with a terribly hard, cold, arctic wind and snow. The temperature dropped like a rock, 30 degrees, in a matter of a few minutes. The snow was so thick you couldn't see, it was a complete whiteout. A bright sun had been overhead and in less than half an hour, you could not see a hand before your face. Chris was at school, they should have still been there when the storm hit at that time of day. When he didn't get home, Louie wasn't concerned because a huge would pile was cut at the schoolhouse so the children could stay there in case of bad weather and keep warm.

Chapter 7

Chris Lost in Storm

The storm started to let up the next morning, it looked like it was worse than the storm in January 1888, when record low temperatures were set, −65 °F (ca. 18 °C) (−54 °C). It just didn't last as long. About noon, Louie heard someone at the door, it was the doctor from Rocky. "Come in and warm up, what the heck are you doing out in this kind of weather. Bring your backpack in. How can you ski with a pack this heavy?"

The doctor replied, "Good to meet you, my name is Toivo Virtanen, your town doctor. I was in the Finnish Army before I went to medical school. In the Finnish army, you stay in good physical condition, you must, with a neighbor like they have." The doctor said that he had been at a residence further up the mountain, the kids were all sick. He thought he better get back to town because people would need him after the storm. He said, "I stopped off at the schoolhouse to warm up for a little while."

Louie asked, "Were all the kids warm there?"

The doctor replied, "There was no one at the schoolhouse and the stove was cold."

"You said nobody was at school! My God, Chris hasn't come home. Oh, what are we going to do, there must be six feet of new snow. I will take King and start walking that way but I'm not sure what trail he would have taken, there are two or three different trails that he might take coming from school, all about the same length."

The doctor said, "I will go with you and help."

"No doc, you must get back to town. I will go. Say a prayer for me and King, please. Anna, you and Mary keep on praying until we get back. I will take some blankets, extra snowshoes, and the little dog sled. King could easily pull it, and we will bring Chris back on that sled."

The doctor skied toward town, Louie and King headed back toward the school. Louie recalled there were more trees on two of the trails, he was trying to get a picture in his head of each trail. *Which one had the fewest trees?* That should be the one Chris would have taken in good weather, so he started down that trail. He had gone over a mile on snowshoes, that was a slow hard mile. Being in good shape, he was moving right along but snowshoe travel seemed awful slow. He kept a close eye on King, the dog seemed to be in a hurry, sensing the urgency of that trip. King wanted to go a different direction, towards the thick trees. Louie remembered that trail ran parallel, close to the one they were on. The big dog crashed right through the heavy brush, but Louie had a terrible time with his snowshoes getting through the thick small trees. He fell down several times in the thickets. When Louie finally broke through the tangled brush and got out on the other trail, he realized King had found Chris and was starting to dig in the snow. Louie got his snowshoes off and crawled to the spot, then using one snowshoe for a shovel he started digging his way down to Chris, he had almost five feet (ca. 152 centimeters) of snow over the top of him. Chris had broken off many smaller cedar branches to make a shelter and then pulled more branches over himself making a secure but not very warm little place to get away from the weather. Louie was scared and praying to God to spare his only son. It looked like Chris was frozen solid, then Louie's heart started to race when he could see a small sign of breath coming from his nose.

He got Chris bundled up with the blankets and tied onto the sled. They started off for home as fast as they could go, Louie thought for a while that the dog would take Chris straight home. As slow as he was going, the dog was patient with him and kept looking back, that faithful animal was looking out for his welfare too. It seemed like it took forever, but they finally got back to the cabin and Anna was waiting at the door. She cried out, "Is he dead?"

"No, Anna, he is near death but I'm sure he is still alive. I think the best thing we can do is carry him to our bed, then each one lay beside him, Mary can lay by his feet to thaw them out. We must slowly get his temperature to come back up. When his breathing improves, he will need some nourishment, some liquids, you better make chicken broth or something like that."

They all stayed in bed with Chris for several hours, his body started to warm up, and he cried out, "Where am I? What happened?" Then he started crying because his hands hurt and his feet hurt, he hurt all over his body.

Louie said, "You stay with him, while I bring in more water. Damp cloths should make his body feel better, starting out with cool and then warming up. Anna, gave Chris some water with an eye dropper." He thought that was good and tried to smile. Chris had frostbite over most of his body, his toes and feet were severely frozen, and his hands were frozen, not quite as bad as the feet. It was surprising he didn't complain much. Anna tried to help his pain with damp cloths. He started to take some nourishment she gave him mostly broth. She gently rubbed Chris's body and his hands and feet trying to keep the circulation moving, to keep the blood flowing.

"Mother, the teacher got sick yesterday morning. About noon, she told all us kids to start going home. The sun was bright when I left school and it was almost warm out. I didn't get halfway home when that storm hit, blinding my vision, not seeing anything. Knowing I could not get home, I went into the cedar trees and started breaking off branches, making myself a shelter at the bottom of one big tree, then crawled in. What else was there to do?"

Louie heard someone at the door, it was their neighbor J. B. Larson. He wanted to know if he could borrow the dog, he was still looking for his two girls. Louie said, "Of course, you can use the dog. I will get dressed and go with you."

He said, "No, you better stay here, I will bring your dog back later."

"John, just keep him on a leash while you're searching. He's got a good nose, he found Chris for me from a long distance away. When you get done, turn him loose, he will come home by himself. We will pray that you find your girls OK. Go and be safe." Louie later learned, the man found his two daughters that evening about dark, and they were both dead just a few hundred yards from their house.

Three days after Chris had been frozen, he was sitting up in a chair by the fire. He said, "Dad, I want some deer jerky, I have to get some meat, something in me besides soup." His feet and hands were bandaged, they looked bad, awfully, discolored. Chris devoured the jerky.

Anna said, "It looks like you're ready to go to work on some good solid food to start getting your strength back. Your dad will go into town and talk to the doctor, see what else we could do if there's something we can do differently."

"Father, I was so scared out there covered with snow, all kinds of images and memories went through my mind. After walking that trail so much and knowing that leaving the protection of the cedar trees would put me out in the open more. I decided to break branches off and make a little shelter down at the base of that big old tree. I'm sure glad I did that, I felt safe and good there for a few hours, then it started to get cold during the night and I started thinking about when we were in Dakota territory. That first year, eating those little berries off the wild rose bushes and digging wild turnips, hunting for asparagus, boy that stuff tasted good! You shot lots of prairie chickens and ducks, then we ate goose eggs that one spring. Stealing them from a mother goose was dangerous and tricky. It was wrong to take the eggs after she flew all that distance and made her nest, then got snowed on and stayed right on the nest. We hadn't eaten eggs for many months, but I still felt bad about stealing them. Those were some hard, but in a way, good times.

"I remembered going with you, trapping muskrats, and then a lot more muskrats up in North Dakota. The time we went to that general store at Ryder and bought a bundle of wooden shingles, the storeowner laughed and said, 'What are you going to do, shingle your sod house?' You said, 'No, we need these for muskrat hides, drying stretchers.' I wonder how many 100 rats you and Uncle Ole caught. Mother, did you get tired of eating all that muskrat meat too? All the time we were living at Duck Lake, seems like all we had for meat was rats."

"Chris, I better not comment on that, not while your father is listening. Sometimes it is best not to say what we are thinking."

"No, I will say what I'm thinking, the worst part was the smell from the hundreds of muskrat hides drying in the house, by the stove yet! I suppose that old sod house still smells like a dead muskrat. It is a smell that is very hard to describe and one that is not very friendly to your nose.

"Then I thought about the bear that killed Uncle Ole, what if he comes after me now, he will just eat me for a quick lunch. Then I realized he should be sleeping in his den somewhere up in the high country. From the size of his track, I hope none of us ever run into him out in the wild.

"I thought about the many people who died in North Dakota and their families, then started feeling warmer and wondered if that meant I was dying. Deciding I did not want to die yet, I prayed that you and King would find me, and that's the way it turned out."

Louie was getting ready to go into town and see the doctor, and he heard some noise outside. It was the doctor taking off his skis. "Doctor, what are you doing out here?"

He said, "I knew you were going after your son, I thought I better come out here and see how you're all getting along."

Louie said, "I'm afraid he's got frostbite awful bad. I hope we all feel better after you examine him."

"Hello Anna, I thought I better come out and take a look at your boy, Chris. Can you imagine, they have telephone in some towns back east now? I don't suppose we'll ever have anything like that out here in the country. You could just pick up a phone at home and talk to me in town. Wouldn't that be the handiest thing ever invented? Hi, Chris, how are you feeling?"

Chris replied, "My body is awful sore and the skin itches, but I can't scratch it, the way mother has my hands all bandaged." The doctor gave him a thorough examination, and then he went out in the kitchen to talk to Louie and Anna.

"Folks, this looks bad for Chris, I'm afraid he's going to lose his feet, possibly his hands too. There's really no way I could do that surgery out here at your house. It would be far too dangerous for him. They're talking about having a hospital in town someday but that's way off in the future. I tell you what, why don't you bring Chris into town, and he could stay with me and my wife. When the time comes to decide on the surgery, I have gas to put him to sleep with and I could do it there. I have more equipment available, that would be the safest way to go about doing this.

"It looks like you folks have done everything right, there's nothing you could have done different that would have helped. If we do nothing, he will have a very painful and agonizingly slow end to his young life, the pain will become unbearable, so I think we should amputate.

"There is only one alternative, take him to Calgary by dog sled, and that ride alone might be more than he could stand. He's going to be very sensitive to any cold air touching his body from now on."

Chapter 8

Deep, Severe Frostbite

Anna said, "Is it alright if I come to town and stay with him? I can help, instead of your wife having to do everything."

"Anna, that would be just fine," the doctor replied. "Mary can help her father out here. You could come out and visit from time to time. I think that sounds like the best idea." The doctor said, "Louie, I don't think the snow is too bad on the main trail from here to town, you should be able to bring them in with your horse and bobsled. I think it's going to be very close to spring before we get Chris taken care of. This spring when the weather warms up, Chris will be ready to start a new life, learning how to get along living completely different ways."

King was in the other room, sitting by Chris in his chair, as if he was trying to cheer him up, with his chin on Chris's knee, big eyes looking up at his best friend. King had a sad, concerned look on his face, he understood this was a bad thing. He was there to try to help make the most of the ordeal and get Chris to feel better.

On the next warm day, Louie brought the two horses out of the small barn and hooked them to the bobsled. Anna brought a buffalo robe from the house; she, Mary, and Chris got in the bobsled and covered up with the robe. They were off to town with bells jingling on the harnesses. The horses acted extremely happy to be out in the cool, crisp, fresh air, you could see it in the way they proudly pranced. It was a pretty picture, looked like a happy family out for a sleigh ride. The consequences and destination of the trip caused everyone to remain quiet and gloomy. Chris was the first one to speak, he said, "Father, I heard you talking to the doctor the other day, I realize I'm in serious and dangerous trouble and must learn to live with much pain. I pray I can get through it."

"Son, you have an inner strength that you haven't tapped into yet, before long you'll be reaching down deep inside of yourself. God will give you energy and strength and a peace that will allow you to do things that you never thought possible."

Chapter 9
Chris Loses Limbs

The Karlson family arrived at the doctor's house where they met his wife Ellen, a beautiful young lady. She welcomed them into her large house and showed them the spare bedroom, where they would be staying. Chris walked in with heavy, warm winter boots on his feet, his mother on one side and father the other, supporting him. Ellen said, "The doctor would be back shortly, he was at the general store. Toivo and I have only been out here a little more than a year, we don't have any children yet, we hope to start a family soon. He went to medical school late in life, after serving in the army back in Finland. He loves his work and is very dedicated. It broke his heart to see how badly Chris was frozen. Chris is lucky to be alive. The Lord must have some special things in mind for him to do with his life. Toivo will give Chris the best care possible, probably better than he would get at any hospital."

When the doctor got back, he gave Chris a quick examination and changed his bandages, then he said, "The next few days are going to make the difference, tell us the story. We will see many changes take place and hopefully they will be good." He told Louie and Mary that they may as well start for home before dark, everything would be alright. There was many tears and hugs and kisses as everyone said goodbye.

Chris had a smile on his face and said, "Dad, don't worry about me, I will be OK."

Toivo said to Louie, "I'll bet you didn't know you were marrying a nurse, by the time we get done here, Anna will be a full-fledged nurse."

Louie and Mary started back home, there were no words until little Mary said, "Father, is the doctor really going to cut off his feet and his hands? I think that would be just awful, he will not be able to do anything."

Louie said, "We sure hope not but the doctor will have to do what he thinks is best, your brother was frozen awful bad. Chris will find ways to still do many different things."

It was a week later when Louie and Mary went back to visit Chris and Anna. He was sitting in a chair and both of his feet had been removed and his left leg close to the knee. Chris said, "Father, the pain isn't as bad now, but my feet and my toes itch and I don't have them anymore. I have no feet, you know I never did want to play baseball anyhow." Louie hugged him and Anna, Mary held Chris's hand then gave him a kiss and a hug.

Anna was crying, she looked so tired, her strength was drained. It hurt Louie deeply, he asked, "Are you OK?"

She said, "Yes, we will get through this, we must have faith that we will get through it for the best."

Doctor Toivo talked to Louis and told him that everything went well so far. "The left hand is frozen worse than the right but healing some as the circulation is better in that hand. They both have gangrene that naturally wants to spread up the arms. That is why freezing tissue is so destructive. A family here in town left me a wheelchair when their father died. They told me to give it to anyone who could use it. I think it would be very handy for you and Anna to have out at your house to move Chris around in. Chris isn't very big yet, but you can bet he's going to do some growing. Without his hands and feet working properly, he will grow muscles that will be unbelievable. Chris will devise ways to get himself around, to do many things that will surprise us.

"He has been reading many of my medical books. He just loves to read he finds the medical field interesting and fascinating. Chris has read most of my books covering the circulatory system. He just studied everything I have about frostbite and freezing and seems to be fascinated with the circulatory system. Reading about treating heart conditions was truly amazing to him. I have talked to him after he reads a book, he retains the information as if it was going into a recording machine. He seems to have learned more since he has been here at my house, than I learned in many months at medical school. Chris has been blessed with a photographic memory, it is limitless, the amount of information he can retain if he continues to read what I have in my library. He gets done with one book and is ready to start another one with the same hungry interest and anticipation as if his brain is starving for information. The other day Anna was turning pages for him, she went to do something else, he just picked up the feather quill that was on the desk in his teeth and turned the pages. Anna was so surprised."

Doctor Toivo said, "Why don't you take Anna home with you for a week? If I decide that we must take Chris's hands, I will wait until she gets back to help with him. I've been hoping we can save them but one more week won't make much difference, she needs her rest."

Louie said, "Thank you, that sounds like a good idea to me." Louie, Anna, and Mary started to return home. The bobsled runners making a crunching noise as it moved over the snow that thawed during the day and now refroze. They traveled along smooth and quiet in the shaded places where the snow was still fluffy. The silence was broken by Anna sobbing.

She said, "Louie, this is all my fault, you would have stayed in Michigan if I hadn't kept nagging you to leave the mine."

"No," he replied, "this is not your fault! What happened to Chris is the results of us living in this world, we had no control over it. Bad things happen to good people every day. This is really Satan's world, it is not God's place, not until Jesus returns someday. It would be easy to blame ourselves, that would make the devil happy. What has happened to Chris, we had nothing to do with, it has happened, it is done. We now need to make the most of the consequences. We all will help Chris do things to keep his spirits up. We do not want the devil to get into his mind and stop his fight to stay alive, to move forward, to make the most of each day. We must support him the best we can when he comes home, he's going to have some very dark days. King is at home right now waiting for him, the poor dog feels miserable without Chris. I know when Chris does get back, King will try to encourage him and help him to move forward too. No,

Anna, this is not your fault if anything it would be my fault for being greedy and wanting land so I could be a wealthy farmer."

Mary said, "Daddy, I don't like it, you and Mom are fighting, I've never heard you do this before."

Louie replied, "Mary, we are not fighting, we just feel bad for Chris, and we're trying to figure out why it happened. That is something we will never do. I'm sorry if we scared you."

They finished the ride home, everyone was quiet. That evening sitting by the fire, Anna said, "You should have seen Chris last week. He was reading books all day long, he would have read at night, but the kerosene lamp made such poor light. The doctor said, 'Chris learned more reading that week than he did in many months at medical school.' Doctor Toivo cannot believe how fast he learns, I couldn't turn the pages fast enough, so he figured out a way to turn them himself without his hands."

The week Anna spent at home seemed to fly past faster than a high mountain storm cloud. She was dreading the thought of going back to town with the knowledge that the doctor would be amputating at least one of Chris's hands, but she couldn't stand to see him suffer. Anna thought to herself, *If becoming a nurse requires what I have done these past few weeks, I don't want any part of it*. She helped Doctor Toivo with the gas when he put Chris to sleep. She watched her boy sleep as if he were dead, and then the doctors started cutting the leg bones with the saw. She would never forget that sound of the saw going through the bones as long as she lived. He cut off the right leg just above the foot after pulling much of the good flesh back, then brought the flesh around the open bone and sewed it up. Chris started to wake up a little, the doctor told her to give Chris a little more gas. The doctor examined the flesh on the left leg closely, then cut the bone just below the knee, well into the good flesh where the color looked OK, he did not want any gangrene to remain in Chris's leg. He pulled the good flesh over the end and sewed it up. Anna was trying to comfort Chris with warm, wet washcloths, his skin felt cold on his forehead. She stayed with him until he regained consciousness, then gave him a kiss. Chris was crying, but he said that he felt no pain, the doctor had used some drug to numb the areas where he cut. After about an hour, Chris was having very bad pain so the doctor gave him a drug to help make the pain go away. Anna slowly gave him sips of water and some tea. Now she would have to go through this all over again with his arms and hands. She said, "Lord, give me the strength to get through this next week. Please, Lord, give me the strength."

She stayed in town and Louie and Mary returned to the log house. Mary said, "I'm scared for Chris."

Louie replied to her, "Me too."

That week the doctor amputated Chris's right arm just below the elbow. The left arm had done some healing; they were trying to keep hope up for that arm. Another week passed, it almost seemed as if Chris read books constantly to keep his mind off the pain he was having. That pain had to be nearly unbearable some days. Decision time came for Chris's left arm. Doctor Toivo said to Chris, "We, don't have to do this if you want to take the chance of keeping it. As you can see, Chris, the color is very bad, and the blood isn't circulating in it. You read about the results from loss of circulation this week. I'm afraid the gangrene will continue to go up your arm, and it will poison you in time. It will take your life away from you." The doctor said, "Chris, in Finland they have a thing they call *Sisu*. There is really no definition for it. It is a combination of things, a strong will, or guts, inner strength or power, each person has it in their body. I believe it is part of their soul. Chris, I can see that you have an abundance of *Sisu* in you, I believe you can get through this and overcome all the obstacles that it will present, but this is your decision. You tell me what you want to do."

Chris looked at the doctor tears in his eyes. "I want to live so much, please remove this other arm. We will leave it all in the Lord's hands, I'm sure he will protect me and guide me for the rest of my days in this world." Doctor Toivo removed Chris's left arm, it was taken off just above the elbow.

Anna had assisted the doctor in removing Chris's right arm. The whole procedure went good, they talked it over. The doctor asked if she wanted to wait a week and see if the healing got any better or if the gangrene seemed to be going away in the left arm. She was all for waiting for another week and got busy praying for his left arm. A week had gone by, the change was not for the better, the gangrene had moved a little farther up the arm. The doctor started to work on the left arm, cutting the flesh around the arm and pulling it back. He made sure it was above the gangrene then sawed the bone off, then sewed the flesh over the protruding bone end. The bleeding wouldn't stop, he had to cauterize it. Anna passed out during the procedure of cauterizing, the smell and the smoke made her faint. The doctor's wife was in the next room, she hurried in and helped revive her. Anna tried to apologize for passing out but the doctor said, "There's nothing to apologize for, it's a terrible thing to witness. I was hoping we wouldn't have to do that."

Chris and Anna stayed at the doctor's house for two more weeks, he was healing nicely. The day Louie and Mary came to pick them up, they all had a party with cake and ice cream. The doctor told Louie that he was going to find a prosthetic for Chris to use on his right arm. That would be a birthday gift from him and Ellen. He told Louie that he was not going to send him a bill, he could pay some money when he had extra, or if the doctor had poor luck hunting, he could bring the doctor some meat, or eggs from his chickens. Louie was speechless and told the doctor there was no way he and Anna could ever thank or pay them enough for what they did.

Doctor Toivo talked to Louie outside of the house. "Louie, last week somebody found a huge bear, they are sure it was your cousin's killer. When it was skinned, they found five 30 caliber slugs in its head."

Louie replied, "If it had been shot in the head, that big bear must have caught Ole by surprise. It must have had him in a death grip, with its huge paws when he shot it. Ole would have shot that bear through the heart and lungs, never in the head. I can't imagine how he could have hung on to his rifle while the bear was mauling him, but that must be what happened. God, I hope Ole was dead when that massive, mountain monster was gnawing on his legs."

Toivo said, "The district mounties think that is the largest silvertip grizzly bear ever killed in Alberta. One thing we know for sure, it died with a severe headache."

Chapter 10

Pioneer Peace, At Last

The Karlson family were all returning to their home together, the sleigh bells were ringing happier sounds. They were returning on a positive note after a long negative period of exhaustion, worry, and fear.

The family had only been home for a few days before Chris learned that he could walk with King, by hanging on to the big dog's neck and walking beside him on his knees. They became an inseparable pair as they walked around the house and yard. Chris was developing extra strong muscles in his upper body and in what was left of his arms and legs. He became solid as a rock.

The doctor brought a big box of medical books from the university and had them shipped to Chris. The doctor worked regularly with Chris's teacher, and they planned a way where Chris could take a test to be admitted to the university in three years. Chris was schooled at home, or you might say self-taught. Chris loved the outdoors just as his father and his uncle did, but he stayed inside and studied the books for many hours a day. On nice days he would take his books and sit out on a big tree stump to study and study, and study some more. The teacher would come to see him every week or two. She and the doctor became more amazed with each passing week as Chris's knowledge grew, he was truly an amazing student, an outstanding scholar.

Chris passed the college entrance examination, then he went to the university. Living on campus they supplied him with prosthetic limbs and a wheelchair, possibly the first motorized chair. He graduated with honors and stayed there and later became a teacher in the medical school.

The province did this because there was a severe shortage of doctors, especially in the isolated rural areas of all the provinces. Most who graduated from medical school, wanted to work in metropolitan areas. Few new doctors chose the rural communities to work in for economic reasons, the people were poorer, they had little money to pay them with. It was a bold move that proved to work and supplied doctors: good, faithful doctors, to serve the rural communities.

Ole Olson (My great-grand-father) at Crimson Lake, Alberta

Ole Olson helping free a snowed in train in Alberta, Canada

.

CPSIA information can be obtained
at www.ICGtesting.com
Printed in the USA
LVHW051237180723
752689LV00005B/42

9 781645 753957